Azucena

Azucena

CENTENNIAL
EDITION

POEMS BY

M. de Gracia Concepción

A Karen & Michael Braziller Book

PERSEA BOOKS / NEW YORK

PERSEA BOOKS, INC.
90 Broad Street
New York, New York 10004

Library of Congress Control Number: 2025946172

Book design and composition by Rita Skingle
Typeset in Hoefler Text
Manufactured in the United States of America. Printed on acid-free paper.

CONTENTS

INTRODUCTION

A Wayward Poet: The Life of Marcelo de Gracia Concepción

by Emmanuel David

In late autumn 1924, Marcelo de Gracia Concepción walked into the Putnam Bookstore at 2 West 45th Street in Midtown Manhattan with a manuscript in hand. "I was in an adventurous mood," recalled Concepción. He struck up a conversation with one of the store managers, who, after learning that Concepción was a poet, took him up to the office of G.P. Putnams & Sons on the second floor, where he pitched to an editor what would become his first volume of poetry.[1] "I placed in his hands the disconnected papers I had to offer," Concepción later wrote in a letter. "I was shy and expected defeat. I had been advised and warned beforehand by experienced men in the field. I was prepared, however, with hardened courage to receive them back. I hardly knew how to breathe during the fatal hours."[2]

Within one week, Concepción had signed a contract for the publication of what he called a "modest volume of improvident little pieces." Reflecting on this episode, he wrote, "I am happy, although the sudden consummation of the thing amazed me. I never expected that so tried and eminent a house should have been so taken, perhaps, at a moment of weakness."[3]

Bearing the title *Azucena*, the name of a fragrant white flower in the Philippines, Concepción's book was published in August 1925. As the *New York Times Book Review* noted at the time, it was the "first volume of English poetry to be written by a Philippine poet" in the United States.[4] Concepción had defied the odds facing immigrant writers by landing a book deal with a leading press, paving the way for other Filipino writers in the U.S. and proving wrong the detractors who had long insisted that he would never sell his work in the American marketplace.

Azucena is a slim volume, fifty-six pages bound in green cloth and enclosed by an unassuming dustjacket with only the title on the cover and a short biographical entry on the front and end flaps. The book contains nineteen poems that evoke haunting twilight landscapes, lost loves, and the power of poetry. In his foreword, Concepción introduces himself to the literary world as a "wanderer," a writer far from home, one who "chose the English language as company." He had come of age during the American colonial period in the Philippines, which was taken from Spain by the United States at the end of the Spanish-American War in 1898. His poems and foreword gave U.S. audiences one of the first glimpses into the world of a literary subject from "their" relatively new colony.

Concepción's foreword provided readers with elements that would later frame his literary reception in the United States by listing as his influences, in addition to Edgar Allan Poe, the work of Lafcadio Hearn and Rabindranath Tagore. At a moment of increasing contact between East and West, he presented himself as following the example of these writers who had introduced Americans to ideas and themes from the "Orient." These comparisons seemed to have been effective. *Azucena* was reviewed widely, and it was often interpreted as the product of a transnational, colonial subject and read through the lens of Western preconceptions of Asia. Besides focusing on the literary aspects of his poetry, American reviewers commented on his status as an immigrant and the foreignness of his English. One reviewer detected in *Azucena* "a delicate, exotic flavor that is decidedly non-Anglo-Saxon,"[5] while another found that, although Concepción's poems achieved "a certain cadence and melody that is seldom caught and sustained by the would be Whitmans of contemporary poetry," it was "not the form [. . .] that arrests attention so much as [. . .] its philosophy that combines the melancholy of Shelley with the joy and freshness of Wordsworth in the haunting and lovely language of the East."[6] The New-York-based Indian journalist Syud Hossain offered this praise: "We cannot render greater honor to the young poet than to say that he belongs, by his inspiration and promise, to that category of exponents of Eastern thought and aspiration in which Noguchi, Tagore and Gibran are the veterans."[7]

Azucena is emphatically the work of a diasporic subject. The text is shaped by an intense melancholia and dominated by an affective register felt by many in the Philippine diaspora both then and now, in which the poet "feels strange himself. Seemingly out of place. Seemingly miscarried by the current of time," as Concepción puts in his foreword. The poems describe an incessant longing for *ili na*, an Ilocano phrase that means "hometown." Everyday sights and sounds remind him of home and transport him to the Philippines. While Concepción writes of memory and nostalgia in English verse for American audiences, one poem in particular, "Sampaguita," accomplishes this effect for Filipinos with its title alone. The fragrant, star-shaped sampaguita is well known among Filipinos for its beauty and would become the Philippine National Flower in 1934, nearly a decade after this collection was first published. For me this poem—whose first line reads, "Sampaguita was her name"—is set apart from the rest of the work in the collection, a simple yet powerful instance of addressing those in the Philippine diaspora directly by evoking a sense of place through the mere mention of a sweet and redolent flower. Concepción's incessant longing for home continued throughout his life, even as his attention shifted from poetry to political causes like economic justice, antifascism, and Philippine independence.

Azucena was important for generations of Filipino and Filipino-American writers, including Carlos Bulosan, who described Concepción as the "only genuine Filipino poet."[8] His work remains part of the canon in the Philippines, where it appears in literary anthologies and in high-school textbooks.[9] But his fame in the U.S. was short lived, and today he remains a largely forgotten figure in American literary history. And even in the Philippines, his biography and the extent of his literary and journalistic writing are mostly unknown. This centennial reissue of *Azucena* aims to reintroduce Concepción to new audiences of diasporic literature.

* * *

I first learned of M. de Gracia Concepción from my paternal grandmother, Purita D. David (née Purita Concepción Directo), who was Concepción's niece and came from the same town, Santa Maria, in the northern Philippine province of Ilocos Sur. Sometime during my teenage years, in the mid-1990s, she showed me a hand-drawn, annotated family tree that she had composed with her elder sister and that stretched back into the mid-nineteenth century. She told me just a few facts about Lolo Marcelo's life: that he was a poet, that he married an American woman, that he was imprisoned by the Japanese in WWII, and that he starred in a Hollywood film. I regret not asking my grandmother more questions about Concepción, because during the 1930s and early 1940s, they were both in the Philippines, and they must have spent time together.

When I began searching for biographical details and literary criticism about Concepción and his work, I discovered that very little had been published about him since the 1930s. There are brief contributor notes that accompanied his poems in anthologies of Philippine literature, and there are a few short encyclopedic entries, like those that appeared in editions of *Who's Who Among North American Authors*, which described his poetry as "philosophical and emotional, from the standpoint of abstract beauty."[10] Yet, most of these short notes lacked citations or source information, which prompted me to begin a somewhat obsessive search for information about this historical figure who was also my great-grand-uncle. The few details in my late grandmother's family tree turned out to be crucial guides.

Homebound in the early months of the COVID-19 pandemic, I channeled my energy into combing through digital newspaper repositories and genealogical sites, and later, when libraries reopened and international travel was possible again, I pored through microfilm and print copies of newspapers and magazines both in the United States and in the Philippines. I eventually submitted Freedom of Information Act requests for U.S. government records to fill in important gaps. Over the course of several years, I accumulated enough to see that the publication of *Azucena* was just one of many important moments in Concepción's storied life.

* * *

Marcelo de Gracia Concepción was born in Santa Maria, Ilocos Sur, on January 14, 1895, just three years before the Spanish-American War.[11] His mother was Lorenza de Gracia, and his father, whose surname was Chua, was a Chinese merchant from Xiamen. Chua converted to Catholicism in 1899 at the age of 44 and adopted the surname of his godfather, Apolinario Concepción, who was Santa Maria's parish priest and military chaplain. In accordance with Church policies on intermarriage, Marcelo's parents were only allowed to marry after Chua's baptism, and it was then that Marcelo's last name, which had been de Gracia, was changed to Concepción. Following naming practices used in the Philippines that adapted Anglo and Spanish customs, his mother's surname became his middle name.[12]

Concepción was a member of the first generation of Filipinos to come of age under American rule. The earliest documented episode in his life is his enlistment in the U.S. Navy in July 1918. He served as a mess attendant on a ship stationed in the Philippine port of Cavite before being assigned to receiving ships in Puget Sound and then, finally, in San Francisco, where he ended his active service on January 21, 1919 after requesting to be discharged so that he could study at the University of Southern California.[13]

But instead of enrolling at USC, he began attending the University of Washington in fall 1919 (after a summer working at a salmon canning factory in Alaska[14]), where he was a member of the Filipino Club and the Cosmopolitan Club.[15] By December of that year he made his way from Seattle to Los Angeles to deliver a lecture, "Rizal's Last Thought," as part of a literary and musical program at Blanchard Hall marking the twenty-fourth anniversary of the death of the Philippine writer and national hero Jose Rizal, who was executed in 1896 by the Spanish for his pro-independence stance.[16] It seems that Concepción took a liking to Los Angeles, and in 1920, he was a student for two terms at the newly established Southern Branch of the University of California, which would become the University of California at Los Angeles in 1927. There, he participated in student organizations like the debate club Agora and the Manuscript Club, mingling with other aspiring intellectuals and writers.[17] In the early 1920s, his first poems, essays, and book reviews were published in venues like the *Overland Monthly*, the *Los Angeles Record*, and the Los Angeles *Daily News*.[18]

During Concepción's time in California, he began to attract the interest of journalists and editors, including the *Daily News* columnist Martha Foley, who introduced one of his articles as "doubly interesting because it is written by M. de Gracia Concepción, the Philippine poet, and reveals the reaction of an Oriental literary mind to American verse."[19] Another writer who took notice of Concepción was the *Los Angeles Evening Record* columnist Don Ryan, who wrote a series of articles about him in summer 1924. Describing Concepción as a "young Eurasian of marked talent" whose prose poems "smack of Baudelaire," Ryan commented on the fact that while some of Concepción's work had already made its way into print, he was in fact swimming against the literary current and risked having to lead a life of poverty, hunger, and unemployment. "There is a very small market in American magazines for prose poems," Ryan wrote of Concepción.[20] Ryan found that Concepción "handles the English words with a dignified aloofness that refines them into beauty," but also claimed that "there is no chance of his ever selling anything he writes to American magazine editors."[21]

Concepción managed to support himself during this period through menial work with little status and low pay (i.e. dishwasher, postal clerk), but Ryan's account confirms what other sources suggest: that he found it difficult to find jobs. The column makes explicit the role of anti-Asian racism in the poet's struggles for employment:

> Who would want a boy in the kitchen named M. de Gracia Concepción? Under the crusted minds of the patriotic citizens whom he accosts on his daily rounds [looking for employment] stir serpents of distrust. It was a misfortune of the slight, dark youth with the liquid brown eyes, to be born in the Philippines [. . .]. The melancholy of the poet through which his teethy smile shines out to arouse distrust in the solid American citizens for whom he would like to work.[22]

Although Ryan praises Concepción's poetry, his columns are not free of the racism that he projects onto potential employers and editors. His columns move from a racialized reading of Concepción's poetry (as "palely radiant with a light that sifts through a tinted, oriental screen") to a chilling, aestheticized image of Concepción being lynched:

> In case the United States ever comes to blows with Japan over the immigration law, M. de Gracia Concepción will probably be one of the first Asiatics to be lynched in Los Angeles. He is small and would offer no resistance. Besides, he would be thinking of more interesting things—of the wind-rider in the fullness of the moon—of the wayward beauty that sings to him in the imagined voice of the flute that is heard when the night is shrouded with purple mists of scents, faint and elusive as musk.[23]

If these are the words of one of Concepción's biggest early supporters, it is not hard to imagine his difficulties as a young Filipino writer searching for work and for venues for his poetry.

In August 1924, Ryan recounts how Concepción approached him while he was having breakfast at a Japanese restaurant. "I think you ought to go to New York," Ryan reports saying to the poet, "Ship out on one of the vessels going through the canal. I'll give you a letter. And when you get to New York you're almost certain to land a job as a houseboy. The apartment houses there are glad to get Filipino help." After Concepción wonders if he would have a better chance of success in New York, Ryan says, "You know the situation here. Nobody will employ you because you look too much like a Japanese."

Over breakfast, Concepción inquired about the status of one of his manuscripts that he had left with the journalist the previous June. "I was ashamed to say that I hadn't even read it," Ryan wrote, "But I knew without reading what it would be like. It would be like nothing except M. de Gracia Concepción. A poetic soul—a heritage of culture from mingled bloods—a student—dreamer who had chosen the strange medium of English from which to weave his peculiar phantasies." Ryan then asks Concepción if he would go to New York if one of his poems were published, and the column ends by quoting Concepción's response: "Certainly—yes," followed by his prose poem, reprinted in *Azucena*, titled "Ephemera and a Song."[24]

* * *

When the first class of University of California, Southern Branch students graduated in 1925, Concepción was not among them. He had cut short his formal education. Shortly after the encounter with Ryan at the Los Angeles restaurant, Concepción moved to New York. Within three months' time, his luck had changed. He landed his book deal based on the poems that he had mostly composed as an undergraduate.

By the time of *Azucena*'s publication, Concepción already seems to have immersed himself in New York's intellectual and creative circles, especially among those who were grappling with shifting geo-political and cultural relations between Asia and the

West. A few years before José García Villa earned the title of the "Pope of Greenwich Village" because of his connections with literary names like Tennessee Williams, Richard Eberhart, Gore Vidal, and Elizabeth Bishop, Concepción was frequenting an earlier generation of writers and intellectuals that included Mary Austin, Konrad Bercovici, Whit Burnette, Witter Byner, Martha Foley, Kahil Gibran, John G. Neihardt, and Mark Van Doren.[25]

In the year after the publication of *Azucena*, Concepción used his newfound fame to support the movement for Philippine independence from the United States.[26] Much of the literary attention given to Concepción focused on the form and content of his poetry, but his life's work was also decidedly political. He became a vocal critic of the U.S. presence in the Philippines, advocating for Philippine independence in his public talks, as in one lecture in Maine in December 1926: "If America holds the Philippines mainly to bleed it of its resources, or, because of its potential location in the center of trade, and either way, if we be compelled to stay, not wishing to stay, because we have offered our simple friendship, and you accepted it only because of the pearls and diamonds on our fingers, then we are not fit to be of the same household; and we can never be friends as friendships were deemed among the ancients."[27] He concluded that the natural course of development for the Philippines would be for the United States to "give us the grace of your leave" so as to "let us live."[28]

Throughout the 1920s, Concepción's attachment to the Philippines remained strong, and he continued to publish his poems and essays in venues like *Commonweal* and the *New York Times*.[29] In February 1930, he wrote about the University of Santo Tomas in Manila, a place where he dreamed of teaching, as he told journalists and audiences when he lectured.[30] A month later, in March 1930, Concepción left New York City, portable typewriter in tow, on his way to the Philippines, where he planned to participate in the Philippine Independence movement. Penniless, he made his way west by writing newspaper articles here and there and by negotiating with transportation companies to produce freelance writing in exchange for bus fares. "The spell of poverty has driven me from one place to another," he told a journalist at the *Los Angeles Record*. "I have been obliged, perforce, to be on the road like a beggar."[31]

Along the way, his stops included St. Louis and Kansas City, where he visited with one of his "staunchest friends," the American writer and poet John G. Neihardt, who wrote upon Concepción's departure, "Those who have been privileged to know the man and feel his rare spirit will not forget him."[32] From the Midwest, Concepción made his way through the American Southwest, stopping briefly in Albuquerque, where he wrote back to Neihardt to thank him for his friendship and to reflect on his travels. Even though he was excited about seeing a new landscape for the first time, his nostalgia ran deep, something that will not surprise readers of *Azucena*. Everything seemed to remind him of home. "New Mexico is indeed a country for which my soul answers," he reflected. "It is like a dream—and projected, I feel, into a world familiar to me in my childhood."[33]

In California, Concepción spent time both in Los Angeles and Stockton, where he worked on the editorial staff for *The Three Stars* (1928–1932), a Filipino newspaper describing itself as supporting the "cause of Filipino welfare." The editorial page entries during that period tackled pressing issues facing Filipinos, including the Independence Missions to Washington and the 1930 proposal of a Filipino-Exclusion Measure (which was rejected by the Senate), which would have instated a two-year suspension of immigration from the Philippines. In response, the editors took the bold position that "the American people should haul down the American flag from the Philippines if they mean real exclusion." This body of writing is a yet untapped resource that provides a window into Concepción's political views and broad influence among Filipino American communities. His visibility as editor of a Filipino newspaper led to invitations to speak about the Philippines and its struggle for independence.[34]

The late 1920s and early 1930s were a period of widespread anti-Filipino sentiment on the West Coast that often led to violence.[35] He did not remain untouched by this. In June 1931, a phone call was received at a Los Angeles police station reporting an altercation at a Filipino restaurant between a Filipino and a Chinese person. When the police arrived, the officers approached Concepción, who was having dinner inside, "took hold of his arm, shook him and even to the extent of pushing him back and forth without asking who the name of the man they were manhandling was," a process that was repeated several times, "until the eyes of the innocent victim bulged in extreme pain." The officers then "shoved the author to a police car" and brought him to the police station.[36] He was eventually released after explaining who he was and convincing them of his innocence.

It could have been worse. Just a few weeks earlier, *The Three Stars* published an editorial, "Police Wanton Disregard for Human Life," which focused on Agapito Corambao, a Filipino who was "brutally shot and killed in COOL BLOOD and without due warning by two 'brave' Los Angeles cops whose sworn duty is to protect the lives of the innocent."[37]

This experience must have hastened Concepción's desire to return to the Philippines, which he was soon able to do. On July 11, 1931, after twelve years in the U.S. and just a few weeks after his violent encounter with L.A. police, Concepción boarded the S.S. President Jefferson in Seattle bound for Hong Kong; from there he rode aboard the President Grant to Manila, where he would live until the end of World War II.[38]

After returning to Manila, Concepción quickly became active in the publishing world, producing both literary works and political commentary. Over the next decade or so, he worked as a journalist and as an editor at several newspapers, including *The Critic* and *The Vanguard*, the official publication of the League for the Defense of Democracy. Within a few months of landing in the Philippines, he also launched a new magazine, *The Bystander*, which according to one reviewer, was "filled with pungently written, iconoclastic articles, largely about the foibles of Manila today."[39]

In 1932, one year after returning to the Philippines, Concepción published *Bamboo Flute*, his second and final collection of poems.[40] Around this time he met and then later married Elisabeth "Elsie" Latsch (1893–1994), a German-American librarian from New York who worked at the Scientific Library at the Bureau of Science in Manila from 1933–1935 and then later took up a position as a social worker at the Manila YWCA.[41] Throughout their time in the Philippines, the couple helped shaped the intellectual and literary community of Manila; Elsie Latsch, too, was a published writer, contributing columns and serving as the business manager for a children's magazine, which also published Concepción's poems.[42]

In 1933, Concepción was an invited participant in the Philippine Senate President Manuel Quezon's Independence Mission to Washington D.C., which sought to negotiate the terms of Philippine independence from the U.S. Concepción joined this mission because he was in the middle of co-writing a biography on Quezon, and probably also because of his public political stance on Philippine independence.[43] The U.S. Congress passed the Philippine Independence Act in March 1934 and a year later, in 1935, the semi-autonomous Philippine Commonwealth was established, with Quezon elected as its first president. The Act proposed an independent nation after a ten-year transition period. That same year, Concepción and his collaborator Isabelo P. Caballero published their biography of Quezon. But according to one source, Concepción soon defected from the Quezonites and joined the Sakdalistas, an anti-imperialist movement supportive of Filipino nationalism, agrarian socialism, and immediate independence of the Philippines.[44]

Around this time, the married couple joined the League for the Defense of Democracy. He soon became the organization's chairman, while she served as the business and circulation manager of the *Vanguard*, the organization's newspaper. The League supported a number of antifascist causes, particularly around Japanese aggression in China, and the "emancipation of the workers through democratic and not through dictatorial means" (and after World War II, it was characterized by the Philippine government as a Communist front group).[45] The League joined rallies, aiming to break down what they saw as the artificial divisions between intellectual circles and the working class, something that produced commentary in local papers as it was "stirring to see something of the cream of the cognoscenti out in the streets marching hand in hand with the oppressed sons of toil."[46] The same column quoted a participant's statement in a Manila demonstration of nearly 10,000 workers, who stated the group's goals: "March shoulder to shoulder with the workers, rub elbows with them, listen to the terrible honesty of their speech, and discover that, man to man, they are indeed the salt of the earth. Then, perhaps, you may understand what words like social justice, and doing justice to every man, and even democracy itself really mean. Their deeper significance will be reversed to you in a burst of blinding light."[47] The testimony is unattributed, but sounds like Concepción's writing from the period.

For several years, the League continued to participate in the broader labor movement and in antifascist organizing, calling on the U.S. to drop its support of Japan's military involvement in China. At one May Day parade in Manila, the group held placards with messages like "Boycott Japanese Goods," "Beware of Japanese Fascism," and "Use Philippine Army Against Japanese Penetration of Davao." The placards were confiscated by Manila police after complaints were lodged by the Japanese Consulate.[48]

In the second half of the 1930s, Concepción was at the center of a thriving literary and artistic community. In early December 1937, he and his wife opened the Ivory Tower, a bookshop, café, and art gallery in the Paco neighborhood of Manila (at 1225 Herran Street, next door to their residence). It became a gathering place for young poets, writers, artists, and musicians to discuss the pressing issues of the period over waffles and hot drinks. The influential painter Victorio Edades agreed to hang one of his best works there for the opening, and he encouraged other artists in the Thirteen Moderns group to do so as well. The Thirteen

Moderns held regular meetings there, as did a wide circle of intellectuals and writers, including University of the Philippines President Jorge Bocobo, writer I.P. Caballero, art critic and Philippine antique collector Gilbert Perez, and journalists like F.B. Icasiano, Alfredo Saulo, Federico Mangahas, and Salvado P. Lopez. There were weekly book chats in which speakers would review recently published texts and then lead lively discussions, and Concepción and his wife set up a free lending library. It was a bohemian haven where people discussed politics, art, literature, and ideas.[49]

Everything changed with the 1941 invasion and subsequent brutal occupation of the Philippines by Japan. In 1942, Concepción was questioned about his writing by Japanese soldiers and then imprisoned and tortured at Fort Santiago in Central Manila, while his wife, who was an American citizen, was held for several weeks in an internment camp set up on the campus of the University of Santo Tomas. She was released because she was considered a missionary due to her work with the Manila YMCA and her marriage with a Filipino. Around February 10, 1945, the couple's home was set on fire by Japanese soldiers, as Elsie Concepción later recalled in her testimony for the War Crimes Office of the U.S. War Department. Presumably, Concepción's papers, library, and other belongings were destroyed during the war, a fact that has shaped the reception of his literary and political writings.[50]

In the final weeks of WWII, the couple returned to the United States aboard the S.S. Admiral E.W. Eburle, along with other internees and their families who were repatriated by American forces. The Eburle left Manila on April 10, 1945 and arrived in San Pedro, California on May 2, 1945. Not long after, the couple separated. Concepción took up residence again in Los Angeles, and Elsie returned to New York. Still married but living apart, both Concepcións lectured about their wartime experiences.

In Los Angeles, Concepción was taken in with open arms by Raphael and Alfreda Pena, who offered him a room in their home at 309 North Union Avenue in what is now Historic Filipinotown.

The Pena family were from Concepción's hometown of Santa Maria, and they were pillars of the Filipino community in Los Angeles—they were founding members of the St. Columban Filipino Catholic Church, and along with other Angelenos from Santa Maria, they started the Santa Maria Association, which seems to have been a mutual aid group. Concepción often shared meals with the Pena family, whose children Aryln and Ralph Jr lovingly called him "grandpa."[51]

More information about Concepción's postwar life in the United States comes from his 21-page declassified FBI file.[52] His leftist political stance led me to believe that he might have been under FBI surveillance, just as Carlos Bulosan was, so I filed Freedom of Information Act requests with the FBI for records about him. After waiting a year and a half, I was sent his file, which covers the last four years of his life, 1948 to 1952. The FBI placed him under surveillance because of reports that he was a "local collaborator" with known Communists in the Philippines and in the U.S. One informant reported that Communist Party book review sessions took place at Concepción's café in Manila, and other activities that caused concerns were his participation in the Hollywood Arts, Sciences, and Professions Council and his lectures at meetings of the Congress of American Women and the Committee For a Demographic Far Eastern Policy, both of which had been declared "Communist Cited Organizations" under the purview of the so-called "Loyalty Order" issued by President Truman to investigate communist influence in the U.S. government. Concepción's membership in the Communist Party could not be confirmed, but the FBI sought to interview him to determine his views and whether he should be included in the organization's "Security Index."

Special agents and at least eight informants followed Concepción very closely, reporting on his attendance at meetings of Communist Cited Organizations and on his statements that were deemed unloyal to the United States. One FBI informant reported that Concepción "frequently praised the Soviet

Union as being superior in all respects," while another quoted Concepción as saying that he "hoped for the complete overthrow of the United States' influence and exploitation of the Philippine Islands in the near future."

The report shows that the FBI also exchanged information with the office of the Immigration and Naturalization Service in Los Angeles, which issued a warrant of arrest for Concepción in 1948 and sought to deport him under the Immigration Act of 1918. Documents at the end of his file indicate that in June 1952 he was arrested by the INS and then released on one thousand dollars bail. As he waited for his deportation hearing, he sought support from the Philippine Consul in L.A., and Long Beach congressman Clyde Doyle introduced a bill in Congress seeking to prevent Concepción's deportation by making him a permanent resident.

Throughout this period, Concepción continued to write and live modestly in Los Angeles, working as a travel agent at the Philippine Travel and Tourist Bureau on South Broadway. Some reports suggest he also managed a second-hand bookstore and secured music gigs playing guitar at nightclubs. In 1952, he played a part as an elderly Tibetan lama in the Hollywood film *Storm Over Tibet*. Concepción appeared in a speaking role with the main actors in three separate scenes, each of which included extended dialogue. A pivotal character, Concepción even spoke the final line of the film.[53]

A few months after the film was released, in December 1952, he was found dead in his Los Angeles boarding-house room, which was "filled with books as well as maps of Russia and its satellites," the *Los Angeles Times* reported.[54] While the newspaper reports offer few details about the circumstances of his passing, his death certificate lists arteriosclerotic heart disease as the condition leading directly to his death. He was 57 years old. He is buried in Los Angeles in the Calvary Catholic Cemetery, which I visited for the first time after finding this record.[55] His headstone is engraved with the emblem for the Santa Maria Association, and the Pena family paid for his funeral.[56] Just above his name appears the inscription "Beloved Grandpa," a reminder of the close relationship that he developed with the Pena family and a sign that he had succeeded in finding something like *ili na* in California.

Concepción lived much of his life as an intellectual and writer in exile, searching for things that must have seemed just out of reach. During his time as an immigrant in the U.S., his literary career was hampered by the harsh realities of poverty, racism, violence, and the threat of deportation. In the Philippines, as a returnee to a homeland still under colonial rule, he carved out a creative life and community that imagined another kind of collective existence, and then that vision, too, was interrupted, this time by war and military occupation. A poet, essayist, newspaper editor, critic, and lecturer, Concepción contributed in no small way to literary history and to broader efforts to advance Philippine independence. *Azucena* explores poetic interiority, but one can also find in this work a nostalgic and decidedly political attachment to place, to home, and to *ili na*, the seeds in his imagination that animated his subsequent work that sought liberation from U.S. colonial rule. As Concepción later wrote about the struggles of Filipinos, "We are a people, we might say, born to freedom."[57]

NOTES

1 Concepción related this encounter in his brief correspondence with Martha Foley, who would later found *Story* magazine and edit *The Best American Short Stories* for decades. See Martha Foley, "Books are Like People: Good and Bad!" *Illustrated Daily News*, November 23, 1924, p. 2.

2 Ibid.

3 Ibid.

4 "Books and Authors," *The New York Times Book Review*, August 9, 1925, p. 15. In the *New York Times Book Review*, time was spent not on assessing the quality of Concepción's work, but instead on questions about what pronouns to use for Concepción, who published using only the initial of his first name: "The name puzzled us at first; it looked like one of those names that keep the poor distracted reviewer guessing whether to say 'he' or 'she' when referring to the author, but the publishers are kind enough to inform us that the author is the first of *his* race to publish verse in English. So that's that."

5 "Book Review," *The Tuscaloosa News & Times Gazette*, May 24, 1925, p. 7.

6 Elsie Alexander, "Themes of the Vers Libre Order," *The Philadelphia Inquirer*, March 27, 1926, p. 23.

7 Syud Hossain, "Between Ourselves" in *The New Orient: A Journal of International Fellowship*, vol. III, no. 2 (July 1926), p. vi.

8 Carlos Bulosan, typed notes for his "Foreword" to *Philippine Prose and Poetry, Volume 4* (Manila: Bureau of Printing, 1951), Microfilm Reel 3, Accession 0581-012, Carlos Bulosan papers, University of Washington Libraries, Special Collections.

9 Zoili M. Galang, *Encyclopedia of the Philippines, Vol. 1: Literature* (Manila: Philippine Education Co., Inc, 1936), 305; Teofilo del Castillo y Tuazon, *A Brief History of Philippine Literature* (Manila: Progressive Schoolbooks, 1937), pp. 359–362; Alfonso P. Santos, "As I Knew Them," *Literary Apprentice,* vol. XX, no. 2 (1956): 95–101; Gémino H. Abad and Edna Z. Manlapaz, *Man of Earth: An Anthology of Filipino Poetry and Verse from English, 1905 to the Mid-50s* (Quezon City: Ateneo de Manila University Press, 1989).

10 Lawrence, Alberta, ed. *Who's Who Among North American Authors. Vol. V, 1931–1932* (New York: Golden Syndicate Publishing Company), 602. An updated entry in the 1937 edition classifies his writing as "lyrical-realism" and mentions him as an author of "biographical and political studies" (p. 277) due to his book about the Philippine President Manuel Quezon.

11 Entry for Marcelo de Gracia in "Bautismos" [Baptisms], 1894–1897, vol. 20, p. 96, Records of the Assumption of the Basilica of Our Lady of the Assumption, Santa Maria, Ilocos Sur, Philippines, available in "Santa Maria, Ilocos Sur, Philippines records," *FamilySearch*, image group number 007774698, Philippines, Catholic Church Records, 1520–2014. Concepción might not have known his exact birth date, which may explain why it appears as January 15, 1895 on his signed draft registration card, completed on May 9, 1945 (Selective Service Registration Cards, World War II: Fourth Registration. Records of the Selective Service System, Record Group Number 147. National Archives and Records Administration) and as January 16, 1895 in the Veterans Administration Master Index, 1917–1940 ("Marcelo de Gracia Concepción," Official Military Personnel Files, RG 24, Records of the Bureau of Naval Personnel, National Archives and Records Administration, St. Louis, Missouri).

12 Biographical details are drawn from the Directo-Concepción Family Tree, written by Purita D. David and Paz D. Manzano; the baptismal entry for Chua (Apolinario Concepción) in "Buniag" [Baptisms], 1898–1899, vol. 21, p. 377, Records of the Basilica of Our Lady of the Assumption, Santa Maria, Ilocos Sur, Philippines, available in "Santa Maria, Ilocos Sur, Philippines records," *FamilySearch*, image group number 007775579, Philippines, Catholic Church Records, 1520–2014; and the marriage entry for "Apolinario con Lorenza," in "Casar" [Marriage], 1898–1923, vol 7, p. 70, Records of the Basilica of Our Lady of the Assumption, Santa Maria, Ilocos Sur, Philippines, available in "Santa Maria, Ilocos Sur, Philippines records," *FamilySearch*, image group number 007774699, Philippines, Catholic Church Records, 1520–2014. On Chinese-Filipino intermarriage in the Philippines at the time, see "Catholic Conversion and Marriage Practices among Chinese Merchants," in Richard Chu, *Chinese and Chinese Mestizos of Manila: Family, Identity, and Culture, 1860s–1930s* (Boston: Brill, 2010), 145–178.

13 Concepción, Official Military Personnel Files.

14 Abad and Manlapaz, *Man of Earth*, pp. 367–368.

15 Enrollment verified with University of Washington Registrar and the Register of Students in the 1919–1920 Catalogue, General Series 1, No. 135, July 1920, University of Washington, Seattle, Washington, p. 310. See also "Filipino Club" and "Cosmopolitan Club," University of Washington *Tyee* yearbook, 1920, pp. 449, 451.

16 "So. Cal. Philippine Builders to Honor Dead National Hero," *Los Angeles Evening Herald*, December 30, 1920, p. B1.

17 Enrollment verified with UCLA Registrar. "Agora" and "Manuscript Club," The *Southern Campus* yearbook, v. 002, University of California, Southern Branch, 1921, pp. 84, 113. Concepción is mentioned as an alumnus of "Agora."

18 M. de Gracia Concepción, "Nostalgia," *Overland Monthly and Out West Magazine*, vol. LXXX, no. 2 (August 1922): p. 29; "Our Christian California," *Los Angeles Evening Record*, March 8, 1924, p. 1; "The Phantom," *Los Angeles Evening Post-Record*, April 16, 1924, p. 1; book review of Hazel Hall's *Walkers* in "Turning the Page with Martha Foley," *Daily News*, June 22, 1924, p. 8; book review of Isabel Patterson's *The Singing Season* in *The Daily News*, July 24, 1924, p. 6.

19 "Turning the Page with Martha Foley," *Daily News*, Sunday, June 22, 1924, p. 8.

20 Don Ryan, "Our Christian California," *Los Angeles Evening Record*, Saturday, March 8, 1924, p. 1.

21 Ibid.

22 Don Ryan, "Wind-Rider," *Los Angeles Evening Post-Record*, Wednesday, April 16, 1924, p. 1.

23 Ibid.

24 Don Ryan, "Ephemera: The Starving Poet Sings," *Los Angeles Evening Post-Record*, August 7, 1924, p. 1

25 Author biography on dust jacket of Isabelo P. Caballero and M. de Gracia Concepción, *Quezon: The Story of a Nation and its Foremost Statesman* (Manila: International Publishers, 1935).

26 Emma W. Moseley, "Philippines Should Be Granted Independence Writer Says," *Portland Evening Express*, December 26, 1926, p. 17.

27 Quoted in Alice Frost Lord, "Silent Trails with Maine Folks," *Lewiston Evening Journal*, December 23, 1926, p. 4.

28 Ibid.

29 M. de Gracia Concepción, "Going Home," *New York Times*, May 4, 1925, p. 18. Concepción was also publishing in the Philippines. One essay, "Filipino Poet Contemplates the Paradox that is New York," was published in the Philippines in *Graphic* magazine, bringing his diasporic perspective back to a Philippine readership. Whereas his earlier work drew interest among American audiences due to his vantage point as a Filipino migrant living in the United States, this essay reversed the literary gaze, providing a view of the New York metropolis for Filipino audiences from the perspective of a Filipino traveler. See M. de Gracia Concepción, "Filipino Poet Contemplates the Paradox that is New York," *Graphic*, April 27, 1929, pp. 43, 50 (in the collection of Lopez Museum and Library).

30 "Santo Tomas at Manila," *The Commonweal*, Vol. XI, Number 14, February 12, 1930, p. 422.

31 Ted Le Berthon, "Poet Son of Many Races Finds Respite Nowhere," *The Los Angeles Record*, April 17, 1930, p. 14.

32 Quoted in "A Poet is Stranded Here; Funds for Return to Homeland Sought by Filipino," *The Kansas City Times*, Monday, March 24, 1930, p. 4. John G. Neihardt, "Of Making Many Books," *St. Louis Post Dispatch*, March 19, 1930, p. 3B.

33 Letter to John Neihardt with envelope postmarked April 2, 1930, Albuquerque, New Mexico. The Alvarado, Fred Harvey, Albuquerque, N.M. Enclosed within a signed and dedicated copy of *Azucena*, John G. Neihardt Collection, Special Collections Library, University of Missouri-Columbia.

34 "The Filipino Exclusion Measure," *The Three Stars*, Editorial Page, January 1, 1931, p. 8. See "'The Filipino' Forum Subject at Plymouth; M. de Gracia Concepción of Stockton to Deliver Address," *Oakland Tribune*, November 8, 1930, p. 8.

35 See "White Mob Attacks Filipino Workers," *The Three Stars*, November 1, 1929, pp. 1, 3.

36 "Los Angeles Cops Assault P.I. Poet," *The Three Stars*, July 4, 1931, p. 8. I am indebted to Jean Vengua for first identifying this incident in the historical record. See Jean Vengua, *Migrant Scribes and Poet Advocates: U.S. Filipino Literary History in West Coast Publications, 1905–1941*, doctoral dissertation, University of California Berkeley, 2010. A few months before Concepción's encounter with law enforcement, another *Three Stars* editor, D.L. Maruelo, was also assaulted by two white Americans (though not by police officers); see "Color Justice," *The Three Stars*, March 1931, p. 6.

37 "The Police Wanton Disregard For Human Life," *The Three Stars*, July 4, 1931, p. 3.

38 "Filipino Poet on His Way Home," *The Three Stars*, August 19, 1931, p. 10. The Spanish-language Manila newspaper *La Vanguardia* reported on Concepción's return to the Philippines and noted that he planned to teach at the University of the Philippines; "Un poeta filipino llega por el 'Grant,'" *La Vanguardia*, August 4, 1931, pp. 1, 8 and "Vida filipina con ropaje inglès debe ser nuestra tendencia.—Kalaw," *La Vanguardia*, August 8, 1931, pp. 1, 10. I could not find evidence that Concepción taught at the University of the Philippines. According to staff at the UP Archives, the minutes of the 1931 Regents' meetings, where appointments were usually discussed, are not in their collection. The UP Office of the Secretary and Human Resources Development Office could not locate any records confirming Concepción's employment.

39 "Villa and Concepción Publish New Magazines," *Philippine Free Press*, October 31, 1931, p. 27. This article notes that Concepción and Villa both launched new publications almost simultaneously; Concepción started *The Bystander* in Manila and Villa founded the literary magazine *Clay* in Albuquerque, New Mexico.

40 M. de Gracia Concepción, *Bamboo Flute* (Manila: Community Books, 1932). See F. Mangahas, "Maybe-Native Exile," *Tribune*, May 15, 1932, p. 14.

41 Entry for "Concepción, Marcelo Gracia and Margarete Latsch Elisabeth," in *Marriage Index, 1936–1937, Male,* p. 18, available in "Philippines, Manila, Civil Registration, 1899–1984," *FamilySearch*, Local Civil Registrar, City of Manila, Philippines. Other documents show that Elisabeth Latsch had taken Concepción's name as early as 1933. See A.S. Argüelles, *Thirty-Fourth Annual Report of the Bureau of Science, Philippine Islands* (Manila: Bureau of Printing, 1937), p. 84.

42 Elsie de Gracia Concepción is listed as "Staff Writer" in first volume of *The Young Citizen: The Magazine for Young People*, but in subsequent issues her name also appears as Elisabeth Latsch. A librarian by training, she regularly wrote entries for the "Books to Read" section, and she also published a few freestanding articles, like "Children of the Sea (A Story)," *The Young Citizen*, April 1935 Vol. 1, No. 3, p. 63, and "A Festival for Little Girls and Their Doll Children," *The Young Citizen, August 1935*, Vol 1, No. 7, pp. 178–179. Examples of Concepción's poems in the magazine include "That Funny Cat," *The Young Citizen*, April 1935 Vol. 1, No. 3, p. 67, and "Says Pedring," *The Young Citizen*, June 1935, Vol. 1, No. 5, p. 112. *The Young Citizen* can be found in the digital repository of Rare Periodicals, Special Collections of the Main Library, University of the Philippines Diliman.

43 The prominent Manila journalist Federico Mangahas praised the Quezon administration for including Concepción. See F. Mangahas, "Maybe-Our Best Wishes", *Tribune*, November 5, 1933, p. 14.

44 "Sakdal Head Here Denies Levies Made," *The Stockton Independent*, August 10, 1935, pp. 1, 2.

45 "Laborers Hail Quezon," *Tribune*, October 6, 1937, p. 1. In a 1952 government report, *The Vanguard* was described under the section on Communist propaganda. See Special Committee on Un-Filipino Activities, "Communism in the Philippines," House of Representatives of the Republic of the Philippines (Manila: Bureau of Printing, 1952), pp. 17–18.

46 Federico Mangahas, "Maybe," *Tribune*, October 7, 1937, p. 4.

47 Ibid.

48 "Assail Japs in Manila," *Chicago Tribune*, May 2, 1939, p. 6; "Manila May Day Parade Stirs Japanese Protest," *The Boston Globe*, May 2, 1939, p. 12.

49 This account of the Ivory Tower is drawn from many sources: Rod. Paras-Perez, *Edades and the 13 Moderns* (Manila: Cultural Center of the Philippines, 1995), pp. 10–11; "Personal," *The Tribune*, November 28, 1937, p. 21; "Greenwich Village: Philippine Version," *Monday Mail*, December 6, 1937, p. H; Purita Kalaw-Ledsema & Amadis Ma. Guerrero, *Edades: National Artist* (Filipinas Foundation: Manila, 1979), p. 94. The Philippine newspaper *Tribune* regularly announced the Book Chat series at the Ivory Tower. One column noted concerns that the Ivory Tower was a communist gathering place: "some people we know have stopped going to the Ivory Tower for their waffles [. . .] because they came away with the impression that the place was full of Russians and

communists [...] now they are afraid the place might be raided [...] and they're keeping away." See "Personal," *Tribune*, August 18, 1938, p. 18.

50 Testimonies of Elisabeth Concepción, Records of the Office of the Judge Advocate General (Army). War Crimes Division. Case Files, 1944–1949. Record Group 153 Entry (A1) 143, Box 1115 (40–18), Boxes 1149–1150 (40–82), and Box 1202 (40–1328). In an "Application of Certificate in Lieu of Discharge," dated January 16, 1947, Concepción notes that his Discharge Certificate was destroyed in Manila "during the battle of liberation on Feb. 1945." See Concepción, Official Military Personnel Files.

51 "Alfreda Mendoza Pena," *Los Angeles Times*, March 21, 2007, p. 13; Interview with Arlyn Avery, September 1, 2025.

52 Federal Bureau of Investigation file on Marcelo de Gracia Concepción, FBI FOIA File: 106-HQ-3106.

53 Upon the film's release, Concepción appears in several film stills that were reproduced in newspapers advertising the movie. See "Dissenting Note," *Daily News*, June 17, 1952, p. 13; "Ancient News," *Los Angeles Evening Citizen News*, June 18, 1952, p. 16; "Lofty Himalayas Setting For Drama," *Los Angeles Mirror*, June 20, 1952, p. 44. The film was also shown in Manila at the Capitol Theatre on Escolta Street and garnered attention in the Philippine press. See "Filipino Poet Concepción Plays Lama in Hollywood," *The Diliman Star*, November 8, 1952, p. 9; and Gilbert S. Perez, "A Visit with Marcelo Concepción," *The Diliman Star*, November 15, 1952, p. 9.

54 "Russ Maps Litter Dead Man's Room," *Los Angeles Times*, December 12, 1952, p. 2.

55 Marcelo de Gracia Concepción's Certificate of Death, in "California, County Birth and Death Records, 1800–1994," *FamilySearch* database, Death Certificates no. 20750-22211, 1952, California State Archives, Sacramento; Personal communication with Jose G. Meza of Calvary Catholic Cemetery & Mortuary, November 23, 2023.

56 Interview with Arlyn Avery, September 1, 2025.

57 M. de Gracia Concepción, "Freedom and Our Love for It," *New Philippines: A Book on the Building Up of a New Nation*. Edited by Felixberto G. Bustos and A.J. Fajardo. (Manila: Carmelo & Bauermann, 1934), p. 11.

FOREWORD

by Patrick Rosal

With your patience, dear reader, I hope you will allow me to indulge in an age-old Filipino practice. I want to mention to you a few delightfully personal connections between M. de Gracia Concepción's life story and my family history.

Concepción was born a year after my paternal grandfather, Alfonso Rosal, and in the same province of Ilocos Sur. The poet's birthplace of Santa Maria lies not far across the Abra River from my Lolo Alfonso's hometown of San Vicente. I also learned from Emmanuel David's terrific introduction that Concepción was a member of the Quezon Commission, a group of Filipinos who were to travel to the U.S. to negotiate terms of Philippine independence. This fact made me wonder if he knew my Granduncle Vicente Llanes who was also invited to be a member of that select group of Filipino delegates to Washington, DC.

One other somewhat minor but very poignant detail from Dr. David's Introduction: Concepción—after his decade-plus of living in the U.S.—returned to the Philippines in 1931 on a ship named the S.S. Jefferson. Apolonio Gelacio, my maternal grandfather, in 1929, just two years prior to Concepción's departure, boarded that same boat and traveled from Manila to Honolulu to work as a sakada, a sugar cane laborer in Hawai'i. Further, that very vessel, the S.S. Jefferson, was constructed by the New York Shipbuilding Company on the Delaware River in Camden, New Jersey, at a site which is within walking distance of my office at Rutgers University.

While there are some nifty intersections in our ancestral stories, it's also clear that I'm a much different poet than the author of *Azucena* in many ways. The specificities of place, for example, appear often in my poems, not just particular cities and towns, but exact streets and corners. This is not at all the case for the poems in *Azucena*.

This *lack* of place in *Azucena* makes me want to articulate my fascination with it. Maybe one of the things I'm trying to do as a poet is preserve my own sense of place; or maybe I'm trying to restore a sense of place for myself because I so often feel placeless; or maybe I'm trying to see a place that is a phantom to me or trying to make myself materialize finally in a place—America—that makes me (like Concepción) a phantom; or maybe, more than document place, I'm trying to invent place out of the fragments of my own movement, my own forgetting, my own heartbreak. On the other hand, Concepción constructs a sense of place by leaving it out; there is no catalog or cartography in his poems. In this way, Concepción and I are both curious about this peculiar wish. He calls it nostalgia. I call it elegy. And I mean elegy as in evanescence and invisibility, as in the mournfulness and longing that arises from that invisibility, elegy as the active and effusive replenishment of a figure in language and in the imagination, whether that figure is a lost love or a childhood hometown across the Pacific or a corner of an industrial borough of New Jersey, whether that figure gets named or goes utterly unnamed. The poem is an outline of desire. Though we sound different and our poems project very different energies, the desire makes us kin.

Maybe the best way to consider desire in Concepción's poetry is to talk about his title. In Spain, azucena is a lily, a white flower associated with purity and beauty; it even evokes Christ's mother, Mary (after whom Concepción's hometown is named, incidentally). But in the Philippines, azucena is a tuberose, which is also a white flower and very fragrant, but it is an entirely separate species. My beloved wife grows a beautiful azucena in a clay pot up in a temperature-controlled room in the attic; it goes dormant during the cold months among some other tropical plants she cares for. When weather gets warm, she brings the plant to the back porch just outside our door, and when mid- to late-summer arrives, the azucena blooms. I love walking out and catching a whiff of its slightly creamy, very sweet smell, especially at night when its aroma permeates the air. Sometimes I can't help but shove my nose in the middle of its blossoms to breathe it in deep.

The title *Azucena*, then, is sensory, even erotic. Like the flower itself, the word carries its sensual fragrance throughout. Almost the entire book coheres around a single romantic interest, who is continually addressed. No physical depiction of the beloved appears in the poems, but the poet mentions her eyes a couple times—and they are blue. Maybe it's hard for contemporary readers to grasp how Filipino men were portrayed as an economic and sexual threat in the United States, as Filipinos were blamed for stealing jobs and committing crimes and social offenses, not the least of which was having relationships with Caucasian women.[1] Fury in white communities especially along the U. S. West Coast had already been rising through the late 20s. In 1930, the Watsonville riots—which saw Filipinos thrown over the Pajaro River Bridge and one Filipino, Fermin Tobera, shot dead—were fueled by outrage directed at Filipino farm laborers dancing during their non-working hours with white women.[2] This is the era that I think of when I read the poems in *Azucena*. A year after the Watsonville riots, Concepción would return to the Philippines, not to return to the U.S. until after the end of World War II.

I have noticed how often Concepción makes reference to departures, something that seems to pop up a lot in my work, too. The despedida, or farewell, is a practice of gathering that I became very familiar with because of my parents. It seemed whenever people came to visit, my family made a pretty big deal about their leaving. That makes sense for Filipinos, and maybe especially for Ilocanos, who have spent more than a century leaving home to go elsewhere for work. Our valedictions swirl with the full spectrum of joy, worry, hope, and sorrow because multitudes of separations are embedded in our story. The despedida-as-ritual becomes an opportunity and a channel for an inner life that often goes unexpressed amid the pressures of working and migrating people. While Concepción's poetry does not intersect in any obvious way with, say, William Carlos Williams' observations of immigrants and other everyday people or Phillip Levine's beautiful working-class portraits, I hope *Azucena* reaches people who will think hard (and more skillfully than me) about this incredible document composed in a time when early twentieth-century Filipinos were working, fighting, dancing, and falling in love in America.

I also hope that *Azucena* reaches not just scholars and artists, but regular folk, even audiences who might not read poetry regularly. The themes in this collection, after all, are about love and loss. They sing in such risky and sometimes precious registers about wanting not to be alone. They approach sentimentality, sometimes they charge recklessly toward it. But time and time again, the poet tries to make something beautiful out of not fitting in. It's a hundred years later, and I think there's no small number of people who possibly very much still relate.

NOTES

1 A labor organizer from Yakima, in a presentation to the Congressional Committee on Immigration and Naturalization, summarizes white anxiety around the presence of Filipinos on the U.S. mainland: "Let it be remembered that most of these Filipinos are musicians, and that the character of their music is of the sentimental and appealing (to passions sort), and that the Filipinos dress flashily, spend their money lavishly on the girls, and Chief Mann [of Toppenish, Washington] said: 'They are just as dangerous when allowed free social contact with women as that of the negro when given the same liberty.'" [See "It Happened Here: Mobs attack Filipinos in Lower Valley" by Donald W. Meyers, Sept. 18, 2017, *Yakima Herald-Republic*]

2 I want to note here that in the Philippines 'azucena' is also slang for eating dog. 'Aso' is 'dog' in Tagalog; and 'cena' is 'dinner' in Spanish. The poet Luis Francia tells me that this slang was documented too late in history for Concepción to have intended it, but there's a small part of me that wonders if the term wasn't already circulating in the vernacular of the American colonial period of the Philippines. In my mind, I make space for the possibility that Concepción was very much aware of the portrayal of Filipinos as uncivilized and that he was naming a collection of largely romantic verse with conscious trickster intent. Generations of Filipino poets, of course, would publish in English after Concepción. Among the most notable is Jessica Hagedorn who would write the seminal novel *Dogeaters*, a title that plays on the savage misrepresentation of Filipinos and refers to the dog-eat-dog cycle in the postcolonial Philippines.

FOREWORD TO THE FIRST EDITION

From the 1925 Edition of *Azucena*

by M. de Gracia Concepción

These frail musings find themselves embodied in the English language, a medium of expression not native to their author.

Little did he guess that the waywardness of his thinking would find articulation in a borrowed tongue. He does not know precisely how or when the thought of writing came to him. But, somehow, it tapped him on the brow like a fairy hand; or, as sound, it may have been a fairy voice.

He was born in Santa Maria, Ilocos Sur, Philippine Islands. His studies brought him in close contact with the works of Poe, Lafcadio Hearn and Rabindranath Tagore. Several years ago he came to the United States.

He longed to wander. That is why he chose the English language as company. He longed to feel the keenness of nostalgic anguish for the land of his birth. That is why he longed to wander. No place is more stirring in the heart of this wanderer than *ili-na* cherished at a distance.

And he pursued strange roads with English as his friend. For many a mile and many a year they straggled together, weary. They passed by many a sign-post and found many an inn's hearth cold and empty. Often there were rays of sunshine on the journey. Often more fortunate wayfarers offered to them finer grains of salt.

In the journey he seemed to come across new delights at every turn, to discover beyond the beginning of a new trail. Stevenson wrote something of this in his "El Dorado," beautifully. So he tramped and tramped, remembering the injunction of John Burroughs' "Waiting," waiting for the proper motif whence that Something may wing its release and find freedom in full fruition.

Poe's lovely life and lines early awakened in his soul a minor strain. The lyric effusion of this American truant haunted him and he dreamt dreams of him.

"Why the deep look in your eyes?" one of his teachers smilingly asked him. He did not tell her that it was "Annabel Lee," "To Helen" or "The Raven" which kept troubling him in his commercial geography lessons. He did not tell her that the songs of Rabindranath Tagore had lately come into his young consciousness.

Perhaps the latent germ of his dream-wish to express himself in words was at that time beginning to break the sods of his being. And it would be harmful to dig into the sacred grounds where the frail roots found attachment.

At last his voice is developing its lyric cry. He can now sing his own notes, feeble as yet. Lafcadio Hearn gave him impetus to try, at any rate, to sail upon his own wings, to sound his own chord, to test in its fullness his voice.

Although not of the Orient, Lafcadio Hearn gave himself to the Orient. And here is a young Oriental who feels impelled to express his appreciation of the English language by using it as a vehicle for his Eastern thoughts.

Yone Noguchi introduced the Japanese mind in that wise years ago. Rabindranath Tagore did the same for India. Now come the Philippine Islands. Not a distinctive contribution by any means; but an authentic one.

And he is carried back in dreams to the beautiful sundowns of his *ili-na*. There is the music of young laughters. He well remembers now his old friendships, the long-lost ties of long ago.

There he sits under the shadows of the bells at vesper-time. The scenes are different now. The voices are not the same he used to hear.

He is all alone in the world now, he thinks, for he feels strange himself. Seemingly out of place. Seemingly miscarried by the current of time.

He stands to go. He cannot understand. Tears roll down his cheeks as tears are wont to come when the soul of man resumes its march to die alone.

He stands to go. He cannot go. For the scent of *azucena* at sundown brings back to him the long-lost ties of long ago.

M. de Gracia Concepción
New York, 1925.

Azucena

To a Nameless One

I dedicate my thoughts unto you—my thoughts
that are inaudible, furtively silent—thoughts
that may recede into the dim future of other
mornings without substance or intelligible
shadow.

But you came and passed me by as that of a
song-laden wind of Summer, and I knew not whence
you came and by what name to call the scents
of your songs.

Now again, I feel the touch of your hands that
are as light as mists.

I like to contemplate the largess of a soul
that is you-a soul, delicate subtle dream—
dreamy and plastic in your being and mystic in
your essence just as holy dreams would be.

I remember the infinite silence in which we
communed during our tender hours of leisure.
I remember how, raptly, your soul sought free-
dom from its concealment to reach out to this
of mine that we might walk the trails of one
common ground or else soar the heights of one
common star.

And you went away, leaving me no sound of
your name.

Ah, by what wind were you blown hither?

For I saw you dear girl, in your blameless garb of blue, sanctified, as though you were in the ethereal heavens of some tropical noon. Was it a dream? Better that a dream comes to me to give me thrills of secret joys and to fill my wants with all the grace of your redolent, simple ways.

Memories

I think of her most fondly, although she strikes
one as would a wild bee that had been cast amongst
a bed of thorns.
In the days when life for her was young and
truly colorful, she used to brush my thoughts
with the flutter of her wings in freedom.

She must have thought of me with equal tenacity
of feeling, for mine was gripping and intense,
though clear and crystalline and pure as the
virgin water of mountain-springs.

I have thought of her often, and I would not
want now to efface what lurking kindly mind
I have for her . . . to demolish the dream-
structure that I have builded of her.

She must have thought of me in devout fervency,
and hers was that kindly thought which
lovingly clings with undying faith to the
heart that has always been true and good as
mine was.

In the days past when I thought of her, I
felt a mysterious urge within me to wear a
thing,—that something—which she claimed
was just the thing for me; a thing around
which memories only could place deathless
wreaths of roses.

How, with that thing, I am able to foresee, with uncanny precision of divination, of her coming—coming, yes, coming, even now that she is gone out of this existence; . . . still she comes, I could feel, perhaps, in the spirit.

I know now that it is Divine Wisdom that played the game, when she went away from me instantaneously, as when she came, probably from Nowhere and to whose eternal bosom she must have returned.

When I think of her, I intuitively decorate myself with the "thing." Then I know that she thinks of me, too, with equal haunting feeling.

I light the censer in my altar and from the infusion of its frankincense into my soul, I intuitively feel the presence of two minds in holy communion.

In that Unknown Land, I extend to her votive offerings of prayers.

The Notes of Your Harp

I was heavy with livid sleep, for my mental fatigue was enormous.

You played on your harp the gay strains of youth.
The fire and passion of your melody, you flung carelessly.

There was the soft rustle of palms, and I felt the caress of the noon-day breeze upon my brow, intoxicating as the embrace of your arms. Still, my sleep was heavy and my lethargy potent to break. I knew it all along as you vainly strove to dedicate to me the most eternal of your songs.

You played again and again with untiring fervency of feeling, likening your music to the ceaseless chants of the sea, lashing the wrecks strewn by the wrack of storm.

You began to be weary and your fingers wandered idly on the chords of your harp. There was a note that you touched and I woke to its meaning—you—wondering how it could have been.

Refreshed by the new note you idly touched, you arose to newer heights, capturing at last the sweetest of rhythms.

You poured forth the living essence of your being in the music of your harp and I awoke to its meaning.

The Censer's Glow

My dear, have I not given thee
All that I am able to give?
And having retrieved my soul so,
Given it thee also,—
Unashamed,
Unabashed,—
To soothe thee
Of the pains
That the world had carved
In thy heart?

Thy Love, thy Love—
For that, men craved to slay;
And having slain,
To paint thee with smirching lies
As the Scribes and the Pharisees
Would have men debauch a Magdalene,
A sinner, they said, red-robed with shame.
But Love: that, thou havest still,—
Unimpaired—
Uncorroded by lust,
World's desires uncouth.

I hear thee in thy call;
My soul reaches out to feel thy groans.
And what, if the ministration
Of my hands' unsteady hold
Shall render service
Impassable to thee?
Then, O then, forgive
The shaky hands so bold,

Yet fearful,
Lest, embracing thee
In rapt divinity,
Crushing instead
The effervescency
Of thine ecstasy,
To spread thy arms
In final embrace
With these of mine.

The Phantom

They call me the Phantom of the Night.
They call me the Ghost that haunts
the lives of men
and of the women that men love.
They call me the seducer
of travellers from off the beaten trails
of mighty cities and woodlands,
who return no more to the embraces of their kin.

They ascribe to me
the weird, tantalizing sound
of the wind-rider in the fullness of the moon,
filling the meadows and orchards
with luscious songs.

My voice, they discern
As possessed of the supernal beauty and power
unknown to human throats;
and yet, to some
I have the soft, melodious purling of a flute
made rich and divine by the ages.

But, whether I be a flute or a song,
they dare not trust their hearts
to beat in unison with the rhythm of my soul;
for I am the Phantom of the Wild,
that spells enchantment,
and they are distrustful of my strains.
Yet, unwary, unsuspecting,
unsophisticated youths there be,
who open wide the portals of their souls

that I may enter and whisper to them
the secret potion of Elysian glory.
Among themselves they say I am a Dream.
I am a Dream.
I am a haunter with tenacious mirth and folly.
I live in the thoughts of men
who think they love;
I dwell in the hearts of women
whom men think they love. . . .
However, to both I am a blue haze
like a gossamer
of ephemeral, evanescent, silken threads.

And when they hear me sing at night,—
or play the flute—
when the moon is high overhead—
they close their windows and bar their doors
and shut me out of their lives,
knowing not the beauty of the earth under the moon,
shrouded with purpled mists of scents,
faint and elusive as musk.

For such is the time
when I am bestowed anew into the world,
and the joy of my spirit
reincarnates itself in the blooms of the fields,
and conspires with the moon to give illusions
to those who shut themselves up in harsh reality
but would not take me into their lives.

Only the unsuspecting youths, innocent and unafraid,
live in the jubilee of my life reborn;
for I am the Spring Phantom of Romance.

His Twilight Prevision

Twilight to him is a moment of consecrated expression of the chastest thought in man. He muses and he dreams. He walks along the river's edge among the bare twigs of the shrubs and the trees in the month of November. The starry night glimmers at him. He projects his eyes wistfully in the direction of the Southern Cross, imagining only that he walks among tropical blooms and that every dead leaf on the ground is a rose strewn by the angels.

Twilight! You are the loving, understanding Mother to whom a groping uncertainty of soul must needs turn, that the reflection of the deep Unknowable be faced unto his gazing that he may know. He comes to you, he, who feels the urge of embracing, your mellow, serene consolation. For you are consoling, when sorrow and anguish overtake him; when his days are grey and his nights are dark.

You see him a solitary figure on the bank of the river. He surveys the horizon. He contemplates the illimitable expanse—vague and undefined. Thus, his Twilight Prevision comes to merge—to emerge—from out of the dim distance of his perspective—to evolve in a form, in a smile, in a voice: in a personality, in a soul that is beautiful.

That evening, he walked home, unconscious of the earth he was treading. He did not know that he was of this circumscribed life. There was the freeing of the whole forces of his mind to the high meads of his dreams and he went home to dream of her.

She appeared in his life like a Dream. She went to him with undying smile upon her lips, like a soft rose-tint of Dawn in the month of April. She went to him and spread over the misty panorama of his being, the golden threads of her hair.

You Were Cruel

You were cruel to me that day.

I never felt before the pain of so gushing
a wound as that which you coldly cut upon
my tired, straggling soul.

You went away from me with no compromise
of motive and action . . . sparing nothing—
not even my sorely tried feelings.

Thus, you went away: your head held high,
your feet striking heavily the stone pavements
—somewhere within the meshes
of walls and tangled wires of the big,
discordant city.

You wanted me to suffer.
You wanted me to suffer intensely, deeply . . .
to humble myself into ignominy . . . to grovel
at your feet.

You did not know, perhaps, how great a
capacity I have for suffering, and that the
pain, distilled in my heart . . . would
crush me? . . .

Never! Never!

Pray For Me . . . .

"Pray for me only, when you feel
as if I were slipping away from your thoughts,
pray for me."
Such were your last words of farewell,
when you went away
in the still hours of dawn.

Pale, rose-dawn was peeping at the offing
on the eastern rim of the world.
The ocean breezes breathed
over the vastness of the plains below,
imperial silence: ethereal peace—
and the majestic sweep of the seas beyond,—
what slow measured dirge
the breakers speak along the shores!

And the skylark soon awakened
with the morning glow, trailing shortly after.
There were sparkles all over the meadows
with dews yet untrod
and with early buds of spring yet untouched.
Then there were melodies in the air
for the skylark had awakened
to the awakening of the world
and the world was lovely and beautiful
in all her glory.

The sun had finished his course in the heavens
and the sun had set.
You were gone for a good many moons,
and the years had overlapped many another year

and still my mind kept the faith
and I thought of you.

There was a time when the dawn of your going
did not awaken to the cheer of the world.
The skylark flew,
but never a note of her song
to greet the coming day.

Ah! I remembered—
my thoughts wandered away from you.

I prayed for you when I knew
that you had slipped away from my thoughts.
And you came back to me
in the still hours of dawn—
pale, rose-dawn,
peeping at the offing
on the eastern rim of the world.

Mood and Fantasy

I saw you under the glow of your evening lamp.

In the morning I did not see you
and in the many, many mornings following after.
Neither could you be seen in the evenings—
at dusk—
under the glow of your evening lamp.

Still, I remember you,
for you left the impress of your passing,
the manifold colors that touch my soul
at the faint breaking of my dawn.

Who are you?. . .
A still voice whispered,
"An unknown friend."
A friend?
That, when I think of you
gives me renewed expression of joy
that is not actually felt,
but joy as is dreamt from out of the void.

I thought of you and I addressed you
in countless vagaries of mood.
I sang to you songs that were borne
by the wind—caress of early morn.

I listened to the murmur of the waves
upon the shores
and watched the rise and fall
of the silver sprays of the sea

at the closely receding hours of eventide.
To the moaning of the wind
among the garden blooms;
to the magic notes of a wood-thrush,
I listened.

Your presence in all these things
I did not discern
to strike an echo
to the cadences of my songs.

Yet, once,
I heard your voice wafted by the breeze,
I knew not whence it came.
But I followed it far into the open spaces
and unto the groves of tall trees.
I followed it far to unknown places
under whose constellation,
it melted forever,
into the cryptic silence of the night.

Nostalgia
I

Dusk was gathering.

I remember well, when rounding the college
grounds on our way to your home, the feelings
inspired within us by the placid reflection
of the young moon, as if it were little Pan
playing among the reeds in the still water
of the pool.

An oriole was twittering its melodic notes
among the branching leaves.

"The pipe . . . ," we sighed in muffled
intonation of gladness, and we stopped in
wonderment, with my gaze resting in your eyes
and yours in mine, not daring to know, if we
could be true to our thinking and dreaming.

"The pipe of Pan," I whispered in your ears.
And your soul caught my words in ecstasy,
for in the blue of your eyes which you raised
to mine, was beauty; and the bloom of youth
was on your lips.

"Could it be true that we understood the
portents of the flitting moments? Could it
be realization that shyly darted from out
the dusk, its golden wings?" we were eloquent—
mute to lisp.

An eternity of silence followed there and ever after. There, as we stood side by side,—for how long, I do not know. All I know is, that there is Eternity and we lived in that gracious instant of Time in the Eternal.

Nostalgia
II

You told me that I would think of you.

I did not believe you. With that terrific spasm of the madness to wander, I left you, perhaps to dwindle away... away... away in the agony of tears; to be broken down like a reed in the fury of a storm. Or, perhaps, to find your sorrows consoled in the arms of another in sympathy.

And the call to wander carried me far and wide in regions untrod by human feet. To be true, you were not obliterated entirely from my mind. For even as I walked the distance of the years, I thought of those deserted hours along the lanes together at twilight, and in the echoes of the distant hills, I seem to hear linger the hilarious trills that echoed and re-echoed many times merry peals of our laughter. All these, I remembered. I smiled at them—these youthful vagrancies—and at times laughed at them; and I kept on wandering ever more to regions none ever knew.

Yet, there came a time when my soul felt the pang of detachment unhealed—gaping wounds untouched by your hands. There is something I missed. A call I sometimes heard. I am conscious of the loss of that thing which cannot be defined. It refuses to be known—is elusive to the touch. A siren perhaps. I am more inclined to that belief. I am endowed with superficial, illogical ideas, you know, and you can comprehend my meaning once your ears are attuned to the weird sort of floating consciousness in the atmosphere calling you. Intangible, we might say. Yes, it may be that. It is that and more: it is the All. Or it might have been just a fleeting, evanescent vision, heavenly and beautiful, that flashed by our horizon in our quieter, deeper mood; or, it might have been murmurs and sounds that so moved us that the sensuous delight of our souls could not die.

You told me that you were another being after that. Yes, the change was beautiful—the transition in your life, in my life. We yearned for fuller companionship, yet, we evaded each other's eyes. And, where many times you greeted my offerings of roses with laughter, you then,—after the change—received them with flushes on your cheeks and tears rimming your eyes.

Nostalgia
III

Enough my friend, that life is lived thus.
And how much else!
What more glory is there in
sight? What ruby-red wine is there that we
have not sipped?
And when we had at last trailed the dusty road,
passed by delusive sign-boards, scaled the
heights of adamant rocks in search of the Light;
and when on top of the world where beamed that
Light from afar, naught was there in sight; when
we had drunk deep of our tears and trudged the
dust with weary feet, and laid our dizzy heads
not on flowers but on thorns; when after this
drudgery following the trail that led us and in
despair we found it not—you rebelled against
the illusion and tore yourself from me to go
your own way, and I in pain to go mine. When
with bitterness of heart and writhing souls, we
turned to go the parting of the ways, there
stood the Cross in soothing rays: *I am the light.*

Then . . . it was then that we understood that
the dust we trudged was gold and the tears that
we drank were wine and the thorns along the trails
were roses.

Thus, we pledged ourselves to love and in loving
to live.

Sampaguita

Sampaguita was her name.

Only a short while did she roam over the
earth, and the world of her birth felt glad
for the soft cadences of her tiny feet.

Sampaguita was her name.

For who could have, in truth, contrived in
creation, the lyrical exquisiteness of a lily,
born and fed of the dew when the morning hour
is young? And such is the metaphor of sweet,
little Sampaguita, who came to us in freshness
as the pearl-drops of Summer-Morn.

But she did not live for us for all time.
For the rudeness of the sun, when the day was
high, robbed us of the frailness of beauty
when the day was young.

Alas, you are gone forever!
Celestial Being you are now.
Still, we search for you over all the earth,
and only when the day is young, do we, in
tenderness, embrace you in the freshness of the
morning hour, decked with the pearl-drops of
Summer-Morn.

We Have Grown Tenuously

I find that the mainspring of my early joys
has grown roots tenuously within you,
that what was wholly mine
to bear in pain and to exalt in triumph,
has received doles of pure light,
expressive of the clear translucent sympathy
that is yours to bestow (as of a regal crown)
because you have the mind to understand,
the heart to feel and the soul to divine.

I have the intense yearning
to be always with you
that the thread of life may not end.
In the throbs of your heart
I hear some plaintive undertone of a soul in tears
for the cause of an erring, ebbing breath of life.

There is light in your blue eyes,
light that connotes the divine ecstasies
of twin-souls' realized dreams.

Thus, will ever be entwined
our kindred beings,
for we shall keep aglow forever
the flames of love we pledged to live.

When you came to me,
You came as an angel in a dream.
You came with upraised arms
eager to clasp my tattered self,
to nurse my wounds,

to cool my fevered brow
with the healing touch of your hands.

I am now feeling the needs of hunger
and my thirst now
for such as you who ministered unto me
is eternal.

You marvel with wistful eyes
at the wondrous creation you have made
out of a life that stood stark naked
in the glare of pitiless beggary?

I shall ever feel the needs of hunger.
For, the nourishment of Life that you gave
knows not the satiation of thirst eternal.

Growth is immortal.
And to keep pace with the infinity of your being,
I must forever embrace the eager call for such as you.

Ephemera and a Song

This: in the month of June.

I hear the call of the unknown . . .
It is the sirens calling me
into the fold of their ken.

The feeling is strange,
that, within the heart of mankind,
there lurks the germ of craving and desire
for places and things that could never be—
wanderings, now in the depth of a chasm,
and then atop the grandeur of a mountain,
discerning only a faint and ephemeral outline
of something man can never know.

It charms; it intrigues, it baffles; it haunts,
and its haunting is insatiable and immortal.

But, ah! those times
when we sang the song of youth
we thought would never cease!
I think of them,
especially at this time of the year
when friendship and other alliances,
which have been formed in the classrooms,
or on the winding lanes of the campus,
shall soon, if they will ever,
be severed by time and distance.

To those who go the parting of the lanes
and do not know when to return;

to those who go out in diverse ways,
expecting to return no more;
to those who walk the sunlit hours of noon,
thrilled with the certainty never more to part,
how many times has the tune of the song
lilted on their lips?

The footsteps may wind their way
throughout the lands of every clime—
whether they be treading the white expanse
of the North,
or tarrying awhile
by the verdant meadows of the tropics' sun—
there shall follow in the wake of their solitude
that wisp of a song,
soothing the mind in dreams . . .
of the far away scenes and murmurs
of far-distant voices,
of the bits of breezes
and the golden sunshine on your hair,
of the bench under the elms,
of the lingering sort of ecstasy
at the clasp of the hands,
and then . . . the pathos of the chimera,
when the spell has melted into the unknown.

There will be years . . .
long, bleak, weary years—between,
years that crowd the cares of bygone days
to ultimate oblivion.
But the Fates are not at all unkind.

For sometimes, somewhere,
a voice shall ring in your ears,
a voice that was once dear and familiar to you:

> "You have not forgotten me.
> That, to me, is sacred and beautiful.
> I have sought the world over
> to quench my thirst for you.
> What impelled me to go on and suffer
> the sears of the years?
> I have thought of you always,
> and remembered all the things
> that were yours
> and all the things that were mine
> and all those things we fused into 'one'
> to be 'ours' wholly.
> Ah! And have I not trothed my all,
> loving you,
> and all of yours loving me?"

The air you breathe is surcharged
with the essence of Life.

There is beauty. There is comprehension.
Within you there is vision
and you cry out loud like a madman:
"I am Life!"

Poor, hungry creature, you are not Life,
but a waif, caught in the toils of life.

Let It Come Again

Ah! Let it come again untarnished,
The golden sifts of its light—
The fervency of our joys
In luminous caress.

Let it be the same visitant rays
Of a sun undefiled,
In the radiance of its peace.
Let the mocking-birds
In freedom grace the air
With songs,
And the palm-fronds
Their quiet, nestled home.
Let the honeysuckle, too,
And the old-fashioned roses,
Their greetings be
        The fairest
        As of old.

I think now of the hours spent
In the garden. Close,
Hand in hand with trusting thoughts
        To wave God-speed,
        In parting salute
To a day that quietly glowed
'Ere its final breath
Shot from out its ken
        In the West.

Still, I hear the mocking-birds sing;
Still, the sun sends forth undefiled
        Its golden rays
        My pains to soothe.
  Still, I pace the garden walks
        And there I pause,
        Knowing now
I hold no more thy hands
        In repose.
  Still, my face turns towards the dying sun
        To snatch a pinch of glow
        Of those that were
        That now are dead

And as the autumn sun
Lingers low beyond the seas,
Then is the time,
When I seem to hear you sing
The songs of long ago.

Meeting at Eventide

I think of you at the soft hour of eventide.
At such a time you come to me
wholly as a bringer of small joys
to a life that was once—
incomplete as it was;
and lacking
in any continuity of method and motive.

Fragmentary shreds, detached from all purposes,—
these, I would collect together
in the vain but high adventure of mosaic placings—
these that were born freely and spontaneously
out of our moments together.

I would cull them as it were;
cull them from the mellowed eves
of many, many sundowns that are gone forever.
I would shake the vase
to reawaken the soul of fresh April dews,
reposing within the calyxes
of many jasmines and lilies,
when the spring sun reanimates to life
the golden flood of dawn.

For these are the motifs of my own existence:
the simple ritual, its breath;
the frankincense, its votive offerings—
touches of kindly gleam
on lookouts that are grey.

You came to me at a time
when I most yearned for a glimpse of you,
and you brought with you in your coming
the softly radiant glow of eventide.
My abode was unfit to be beheld
by one of high station such as you,
but you came in with frank volition,
unhesitant of all ill-meanings
that might be imputed unto you
by those who know not the urge of fulfilment.

You bade me go out with you—
out into the open spaces.
You bade me inhale the fragrance of the fields
and the free-air of mountain-tops.
You bade me attune my ears
to the sacred lyra of the skies.
And I felt the caress of all these
and the caress of your touch,
catching our souls so,
that we were left in solitude,
immured within the chaste garden of poesy,
lisping the language of the gods.

When immured thus,
high up among the Olympian grove,
you sighed to me my name
as never before I heard.

There was a tinkle of golden music in your voice
which reverberated to me
many, many times over
like an echo:

sacred tone that gave life
to a name that was dead.

I think of you at the soft hour of eventide.

The Day of Your Passing

In this, the day of your passing,
the blossoms in the fields
sprinkled low their petals
that they might adorn the trailed mists of the meadows
with the vari-tinted au revoir of their glory.
And there filled the air that day,
fragrance—rare and exquisite—
awakening in the heart new emotions,
and giving to life fresh lease of verdure,
making it realize that the world is naught
but beauty fulfilled.

So, we rejoiced in your passing,
as did the Moon in her silver sheen
amidst the eternal blues of the heavens;
and the flowers in the wilds
and the birds that sing on hill-tops,
for they rejoiced also
in the knowledge of your going,
eagerly expectant of the fragrance of your return
at the edge of the woods.

Here, at the turn of the years,
the children of nature are aglow
in their awakening to the warmth of spring's touch.
The buds begin to break their bedewed crystal cells
and turn upward to the early sun
for a dole of his liquid light.
And we,
who awaken fresh to the newness of Life,
fling ourselves in full abandon,

and with sprightly feet
avidly seek the caress of Morn.

In this the day of your passing,
the blooms in the fields
hold high their silver petals
that they may adorn the golden air of dawn
with the vari-tinted welcome of their glory.
And rare, exquisite fragrance
will fill the earth this day,
making it possible for those who live
to renew their pledge with Life,
and to realize that the world
is beauty fulfilled.

At Dawn

I hold fast to the last chord of my harp
in the joy of expectancy.

At Dawn,
When the valley below is rose-hued and the
expanse of the sea is as molten gold,

The sweetly-perfumed air of the grains in
November is as a harbinger of the approach
of your regal train,

And it strikes my cheeks and my brow, ting-
ling anew the ardour of my soul.

I awake newly endowed with Life and I sing
to the depth of the woods the songs of your
praises.

The promise of fulfilment harkens to the
rhythm of waking light.

I hear the melodies of the spheres.

I hear the call of your voice.

I hear the tidings of an era yet unborn
to the warp of the world.

At Dawn, I hold fast to the last chord of
my harp to weave the music of the angels in the
woods in moments of joyous expectancy.

At Dawn, you come to me freshly scented,
For you come to me bearing the joys of the world.

ACKNOWLEDGMENTS

I would like to thank Gabriel Fried, Patrick Rosal, and Patrick Greaney for their enthusiasm and support. I am indebted to my father Enrico David for providing important details about our family history and to Arlyn Avery, who shared memories about Concepción's life in postwar Los Angeles. Historical research and an early draft of the Introduction were completed during a Residential Fellowship at the National Humanities Center, where Martha Kelly encouraged me to pursue my work on Concepción and librarians Brooke Andrade, Riley Francis, Sarah Harris, and Joe Milillo offered valuable assistance. I am grateful to the librarians at the University of Colorado Boulder—especially Beth Arellano, Julia Seko, Xiang Li, Maggie Kidnay-Rouse, and Joanne McIntyre—for tracking down countless articles by and about Concepción, even during the early moments of the pandemic. Eric van Slander helped me navigate the Case Files of the War Crimes Division at the National Archives at College Park. My work also benefited from the support of these archivists, librarians, and other colleagues: Jianye He, UC Berkeley; Genevieve Maxwell, the Academy of Motion Picture Arts and Sciences; Brian Venner, UCLA; Christine Fish, University of Washington; Mark Cel Manalili, Lopez Museum and Library; Joy P. Cruz, Elvira B. Lapuz, Michelle Ann G. Manalo-Eclar, Martian Jinio, Mark Xavier Dumlao, and A.B. Gideon N. De Castro, University of the Philippines Diliman; Venus Ibanez, Rica Marcelo, and Micah Tutor, National Library of the Philippines; Allaina Wallace, Denver Botanic Gardens; and Jhadee Ann F. Pascual and Ren Divien Obeña, Botany and National Herbarium Division, National Museum of the Philippines. A Kayden Research Grant from the University of Colorado Boulder helped fund the publication of this book.

Emmanuel David